Woman Check Yourself!

Woman Check Yourself!

Julietta Raoul

Published by Tablo

Table of Contents

This book is to the hearts of women. The things we think but cannot say. The thoughts we would love to share yet cannot reveal. Someone knows how we feel, but it is such an unpredictable world that you do not know who you can be honest with when revealing your innermost thoughts. There are many of us who are realistic but are afraid. The word of God gives us the hope and the reason for faith to have peace within ourselves and our lives so we never feel alone. Through God's guidance, he blesses us with women of virtue who have survived and can support us along the way. May your hearts and lives be blessed!

How quickly we forget

A woman and a man at a coffee shop—their eyes meet and there is instant communication. Why is there no more emotional contact three or four years into relationships? It seems the more we get to know our spouse, the less we can dwell together.

In a new relationship, a great effort is made to get all dolled up, get our hair done, have our makeup perfect, buy a new dress, use proper manners, and the list goes on. Men may not do as much, but the goal is to impress. If all are honest, usually, things start off with what seems to be a common ground relationship. As time goes by, you get to familiarize yourself with the other's habits, schedule, and so on. Further into the relationship, whether it be two or fifteen years, everyone gets comfortable. Life is so busy, and we get selfish, absorbed into our work—and if there are kids, they take up all our time. We forget the relationship with our spouse and the attraction that started this life we have. We look across the room and do not even recognize the person with whom we share a house. We figure even God understands how busy we are. Not enough time in the day for little things like a walk in the park together.

When was the last time you caught his eyes and he made you blush? Can you remember how long it has been since you have spent time together intimately? Not talking about sex. We get so tired from chasing all needs but ours that the relationship is suffering and dying, but we do not know it. Neglected couples are one of—if not the highest—reason for a high divorce rate. The job is attended to, no matter where we are, at the office from 8 a.m. to 4 p.m., on our way home, we are returning calls we missed during the day, and when we get home, it's time to finish that project. By the time the day is done, so are we. Our spouses have had their share of a busy day too, and we have not shared a polite word except "dinner is ready." This cycle goes on until we no longer recognize the person we live with. We do not take the time to breathe and realize that we are exhausting ourselves.

We need to spend time on our relationships: relationships with ourselves, with God, our husband, children, and not try to squeeze it into our schedule. It is a blessing to have a marriage built from a relationship of God's love—and for us then to be too lazy and try to put the effort it requires constantly to make it a success would be a complete shame and loss. There is nothing wrong with being independent and strong because it is required of us as virtuous women. Proverbs 31:25 says, "Strength and honor are her clothing, and she shall rejoice in time to come." We misunderstand and take it too far. Independent women are those who maintain their individualism and are confident in whom they are.

What makes you think that your independence is based on how you look? Anyone can fake that. Looking well put together is merely a show window. While you are pretending to have it together on the outside, the inside is crumbling, and one day, pop goes the weasel.

Proverbs 31:12–16 says, "She will do him good and not evil all the days of her life. She seeks wool and flax and worketh willingly with her hands, she is like the merchant's ships; she brings her food from afar. She rises also as while it is yet night and giveth meat to her household and a portion to her maidens. She considers a field and buys it: with the fruits of her hands, she plants a vineyard."

Sharing life with our husbands does not take away our independence unless we give it up.

We are called to submit ourselves to our husbands. The word *submit* has prevented many women from being married or from allowing themselves happy marriages because of fear from the wrong interpretation. To submit unto our husbands is to allow us to be true to ourselves and to our husbands, allowing ourselves to be vulnerable to them and to see our honesty and true love, and then, they are able to completely love and protect us.

Proverbs 31:11 says, "The heart of her husband doth safely trust in her so that he shall have no need of spoil."

When God gives, he gives the best. Our husbands are given to us by him when we trust him to choose for us, as he sees who will complement us in every aspect—a man who admires us for whom Christ has called us to be, not who the men think we should be. You must remember that when we trust God in every decision in our lives, he gives us a man who is shown in Proverbs 31:23: "Her husband is known in the gates when he sitteth among the elders in the land."

Couples: Confident and sure of who they are, they make an amazingly strong team. That is the word we have forgotten. *TEAM.*

How often have you gone on a date as a couple that was not a work function or friends inviting you out? When did you last come home to a candlelit dinner—it was just for you and because you are you? Do you remember the days he came home, and you could tell he has had an awful day? Did you run a bubble bath for two to help relax him? Do you recall the days you greeted each other at the door and could not wait to discuss your day? Remember when you watched movies wrapped in each other's arms?

When was the last time you kissed and got so lost in each other that you had to stop for air?

Go back to the times when you communicated with your eyes in a room full of people, and you were the only ones who knew the thought. Do you remember how you hugged each other in an embrace that made you feel alive? Now you only get or give a "cheap" hug.

Your feet only get rubbed when you book a pedicure. Your neck gets rubbed by a chiropractor because of work stress relief. Gone are the days when your hair looked good every day—now it is wash and go.

If you remember times in the past, you may wonder why he has been sleeping on his pillow. What happened to the man who enjoyed his nose in your hair?

Your shopping bags get bigger with household items. You need to buy some sexy underwear and throw out those granny drawers. Buy some lingerie that make you feel even more gorgeous so you can make your contribution in the bedroom. Some massage creams will not be a bad idea, either. If you do not think of yourself as sexy and beautiful, your husband will have a difficult time as he should not have to convince you of who you are. Our inward and outward beauty is something we need to recognize and be thankful to God for it. When we put Christ first in our lives, we are not lacking his grace and inner beauty that is revealed outward.

Psalm 139:14 says, "I will praise thee; for I am fearfully and wonderfully made."

It is a confidence we find within ourselves that then gets to be loved and admired by our husband. No one should expect their spouse to build their self-confidence. It is a requirement prior to relationships. How about some color in your wardrobe other than black? Replace some of those runners with a few pairs of stilettos. Buy a new perfume that will tingle his senses and have him nuzzling your neck. If you do not maintain yourself in the relationship and generally in life, no one will do it for you. We all love to be comfortable, but there is a balance with comfort and beauty. Do not confuse frumpy with comfort.

We can often be comfortable and yet be gorgeous.

Maintaining me

Are you getting comfortable on your couch, making no effort to exercise or, as the saying goes, "letting yourself go" because you are now in a relationship and no longer need to look attractive? Have you forgotten that till you die, you must always be appealing to others, especially yourself? How are you to keep this man from lacking interest if you do not care about your appearance?

Stop complaining of what is wrong with your body and do something about it. Where is the motivation that kept you in the gym when you were single and dating? Unless there is a medical or genetic reason, you can do something for yourself.

When you get home from work, are those faded baggy sweats the only thing you can wear? Yes, you have been in a suit all day, but there must be something comfortable and sexy you can wear. Do you go to bed with that green mask and try to scare the poor man to death? Those flannel pajamas that are too short for pants yet too long for capris—please get rid of them. It is not cute.

You may not think your feet are cute, but it will help if you get a pedicure and scrub those heels on a regular basis—and some lotion daily goes a long way. It says, "I take care of myself," so anyone with me is expected to take care of themselves too and that being a child of God, I take care of the self I've been given. We need to look like we are children of the King.

So, maybe you cannot afford a trip to the spa, but how about purchasing some cuticle oil, hand cream, and nail polish to give those chapped hands a more appealing look? Now when you go out, your hands will not be hidden in your lap during dinner. Have you been trying to color your hair and to this day cannot get it right? Is it possible to include your hair in your budget, find an affordable stylist who can cater to your styling needs, and be creative enough to give you some versatile looks without changing you over?

No matter how long the relationship, we both need to maintain attraction—we are only human because only God is perfect. One of the ways to keep the spice alive is by remembering we want to see our spouse till death do us part. Just think about it. Wouldn't it be great to have him see you as gorgeous twenty years later? Such fulfillment does not come without nurturing; we will not look like a twenty-five-year-old forever, but taking good care of ourselves physically in one step in the right direction.

We do it for our self first, and then he gets to admire us for it. Who wants a life partner who neglects themselves and then must be taken care of as a patient? It is bad enough that life throws us situations and trials—no spouse needs a careless partner.

Trust

Are you the lady who will not let your husband have a moment alone? You call a dozen times a day, and if a call goes unanswered, you panic. You wonder who he is with, what is he doing, and what you should do to catch him in the act. You need to take a moment to think. If this man has been devoted, reliable, and good to you, but you seem to have trust issues and instead of finding a way to deal with your problem, you are bent on ruining your future by continuingly picking fights and false accusations.

Why don't you try being in his shoes for a bit? Unfair, isn't it?

Did you find what you were looking for by snooping around as soon as he leaves the house? He cannot put down his cell phone, wallet, or briefcase because you will dig like a rabbit in a hole. How would you feel if you had no privacy? Believe it or not, couples promise not to keep secrets from each other—but it does not mean everyone does not need their personal space.

It is a sign of respect and trust. If the respect and trust is broken, there are many ways to peacefully deal with it without great repercussion on the relationship. Everyone in a relationship is responsible for his or her behaviour, that is, the trust. Do not give his friends attitude or refuse to give him messages when they call. If you suffocate him, he will one day seek freedom. Let the man breathe. When you spend time together, it will be precious as you will have something to look forward to. Furthermore, you will also realize that you got to miss each other.

Jealousy only leads to a bitter end. What you really need within you must be resolved by your own inward search and contentment. Your insecurities will strain the relationship and drain him. You must be confident in yourself and not seek what should be self-fulfilment from him or anyone else before being able to give any contribution to a productive and happy relationship. No one likes to be suffocated and no one should be.

It is Friday night again, and why is it that you two are always home? Did you think it was a bad idea for him to visit with the men's group? A decision to spend a lifetime with you does not mean he is to have no contact with anyone else. Relationships are about balance—adequate time with you, time with friends, and even time alone, as in by himself.

So, he wants to go out occasionally with his friends. This allows you some free time for yourself. There are so many things to do. Nothing wrong with watching a movie alone, soaking in the tub, or finishing that book on the nightstand. Do you feel like having company? Call a friend and make it a girls' time. We often feel we cannot be alone because we are in a relationship, but are you offended to spend time alone? What is it about yourself that frightens you? How else are you to discover who you are if you are always surrounded? It is also a way to discover more about who you are. Even in our relationships, we need to maintain our individualism.

Does it bother you if another woman looks at your husband? Don't you think he is handsome and attractive? Do you want to be the only one who thinks he is appealing? Doesn't that make you a bit odd? Never thought of it that way, huh? It is human nature to behold beauty; just do not get carried away. What you should expect is respect, total commitment, faithfulness, and him being able to keep you on your toes—the same goes for you too. Absolute trust and complete peace will be the result.

It is also in our best interest to make sure we serve every available dish to our husband. There will always be temptations, but he will know there is no better server than you, and no other platter will be appealing. We must always be on top of our game. In life, you must give to get and invest to get a return. Only with God do we get undeserving blessing when we put all our trust in him.

Your marriage is one important investment; most of the time, you will get out of it what you put in. This is about having a healthy and blessed relationship. In life, situations are of all sorts: Bad, good, difficult, frustrating, and the list goes on, but when you have matured to a woman who is confident in yourself, knowing what you want in your life, decisions become a lot clearer. The options may be plentiful, but your choice is clear.

"Trust in the Lord with all your heart and lean not unto your own understanding, in all your ways acknowledge him and he will direct your path" (Proverbs 3:5–6).

Getting carried away

It is one extreme to the next. Why do you think it is necessary to go to bed with makeup, wake up at four a.m. to wash if off, and reapply before he wakes up? This is not a problem with him—it is a problem with you. You need to be aware of your own individualism . . . accept who you are. Using makeup as an enhancement is great because it is then a choice you made, but it should not be a shield to hide the real you when you feel you NEED it to create a new face.

You are a unique person, and it is hard enough being a true woman with all of society's expectations: What size we should be, how straight or curly our hair should be, what height of shoe to wear, what to eat this year but isn't appropriate next year—it is unnecessary to put extra pressure on yourself.

You may have forgotten the first time he saw you was the day you had to run a last-minute errand and you were dressed simply without makeup. He could not take his eyes off you. So why and when did you feel the need to hide your beautiful face behind a mask? So, whether you guys met five or twenty-five years ago, if he hasn't said or done anything to give you the idea that you weren't attractive, you need to search within yourself to solve the issue of insecurity.

Ask the Lord to guide you, for he alone can restore us within. He is the answer to everything

Psalms 139:14 says, "I will praise thee; for I am fearfully and wonderfully made. Marvelous are thy works."

Do you need to wear clothing too small or keep wearing the ones that are your favourites that are now too small? It is possible to dress sexy and be comfortable. It is a matter of personal choice. But we tend to confuse choice with taste. Wearing our clothes to fit our individual bodies in a way that is flattering, complementary, and confident makes a statement of who you are. The rule of thumb is to expose one body part per outfit. That is, legs are sexy, but a mini should measure inches above the knee and not inches below the butt. Cleavage is sexy, but when you are really gifted in the bust, it makes for a show. What is your personal rule? What do you want to be the first impression? How we present ourselves is a personal declaration.

What consequences are you setting yourself up to suffer later? Each one of us is responsible for our choices and decisions, but have we ever really thought of the long-term effects and repercussions for the smallest things? They sure do add up in years to come. Think of the sum of those consequences as a parent though some choices are worth the consequences resulting in most valuable lessons, as even God allows us to go through situations and trials to bring us out greater for his honor and glory. But those other choices that you know you will be kicking yourself for because they are so ridiculous sometimes—they warrant a head shake.

Let us pay attention and be diligent in the smallest of decisions as they all have an impact on our relationships. It all starts with us, but let it all be guided by his will for us, whether it be our dissatisfactions with looks and a need to embrace ourselves truly or our presentation to this world because as his children, we are called to stand out.

Beauty beheld

What do men, and I mean men—(not boys in adult bodies)—see as beauty?

We often will not be caught with our hair undone, makeup off, or not wearing the attire for the occasion just in case the prospect sees us.

It is amazing how we are consumed with aiming for perfection, but we are so unaware that what we show or fix is not what a real man is seeing or seeking. We believe he looks at our curves, face, hair, shoes, and outfit.

Girl, you are a bit wrong. He sees these things all right, but that is not what they are watching and observing. What he is paying attention to the expressions on your face as he sees you when you do not see him—how assertive or confident your movements and walk are. Not the brand of your shoes, but do you walk like they are too small for you? Do your clothes fit too snug for comfort or do you wear your size with poise? Your hair: No matter the length, color, or cut, it should be worn to suit you with chic elegance or a funky edge—it should not look neglected.

He is looking to see if you drive a run-down car but are accessorized with expensive brands of handbags and shoes.

Are your fingers covered in rings so he knows there is no space for any marriage proposal because you are busy cluttering them up? Are your strides sluggish and lazy because you have had a bad day, and everyone can tell the day you have had, and you have lost the confident walk you had yesterday? Are you always speeding or running because you are tardy and cannot be trusted with punctuality?

You got a stain on your favourite jacket. Is it still there because it will not come out or because you cannot be bothered to remove it or abandon the jacket?

Are you always on the run, getting dressed, putting on makeup, or brushing your teeth in the car? Does he get to notice you jog on your lunch break and is aware that there isn't a shower at work? In the summer, are those feet pedicured from those winter shoes before you expose them in sandals?

Are your clothes looking like a cow was chewing on them, or are they de-wrinkled and neat? Presentation matters. What we think men see are not what they are watching.

Are you complaining about your weight and doing nothing about it?

Are you gossiping or asking personal questions? He sees a woman he cannot trust. He is always listening. How much do you complain? Do you tell him of your personal conquest when you have been out, not realizing he is a potential mate also, or someone he knows? Are you extremely quiet and secretive?

Men (do not be confused by little boys in grown bodies) are observant to what interests them, but most women (not little girls in adult bodies) will not know till it is too late. I have witnessed a man who constantly was in the presence of many single women. I watched the man who was quiet and polite and often came in, and not once did the women take notice of him even though he often greeted the ladies. This man became famous and met a beautiful lady and was married two years later, and it was then the other ladies took notice of him. They then made snide remarks of his choice of companionship. But I often wonder to myself why he would have chosen any of them when he had gotten to observe their ugliness and they were so unaware of his presence. They now thought they were worthy of him because he was famous.

I have appreciated the lesson from this observation on all sides. When you are on the outside of a situation, oh, what a view. So, I am asking you to think of yourself and do not start a life of pretense, but search for the true you or keep working on a better version of you.

Remember the old saying by Saint Jeremy:
"Good, better, best
Never lets us rest
Until the good is better
And our better becomes our best."

Put it out there what you want to be honest, and you will not have to apologize for it. No one is perfect, so if you are aware but not overly conscious of yourself, it will help create some good balance with the results. It is all part of growing and learning. No one can take away from you who you are unless you give them permission to.

Self-liberation

Why are you afraid to be adventurous in the privacy of your home? It is private for a reason. Think of why you and your husband should not experience some beautiful, lingering, luscious moments. Many people confuse sex with intimacy. Sex is the meeting of two bodies ending in the climax; intimacy is an emotion, a thought, a feeling combined by two people, a mental connection that cannot be explained. It is a husband who looks at you from across the room, and you can see, feel, and understand the depth of passion spoken in a language understood by no one else but the two of you. Then when you two are alone, the passion in the rooms makes the paint peel off the walls from the body heat—your breath is so deep that at his touch, you gasp for air. When you look at each other or even out of each other's presence, no celebrities with big chests or pretty faces seem to be able to compare to the beauty you behold in your spouse.

If the two of you agree, it is no-holds-barred. Many relationships lack spontaneity and fun. Yes, fun! Increase the sexy underwear, and add some sheer lingerie, lotions, et cetera. Get creative. Remember when you just got married. What on earth could ever prevent you from allowing yourself to lose the simple pleasures of your life? There should not be a schedule for pleasure and great satisfaction. Do not go crazy—this is not about "swinging from the chandelier."

Line up that lingerie and make a fashion show, but save the sexiest for last and let the fun increase. How about some slow music, and you can really put some moves on him and let him show some of his moves too. That will make for a great day. All you must do is keep your man's eyes and heart on you by doing your share of commitment. See, there is no need for jealousy. He has made his choice, so remind him what a great choice it is. Hey, he was your pick too.

To fix or not to fix

What happens to the relationship when the person you have known and loved has changed before your eyes? YOU DON'T FALL APART. That is what you do. At the end of the day, your individualism will come in handy right about now. We have God as our guide, and he has already given us the tools to survive life. It is all within us—all we must do is dig in and do what needs to be done. "I can do all things through Christ who strengthens me" (Phil: 4:13). If you fall apart, it shows you are giving in to the situation or problems, and the focus is not on Christ who is always on time, and he is our rock and a very present help in times of trouble (Psalm 46:1). We often feel that doing the right thing is staying to fix it or fix him. He is not yours to fix, and you are not his for fixing.

Each adult is to maintain who they truly are, to be able to live a content life. Life changes around us all the time. We want the best results out of situations, so why do we then accommodate the wrong when it happens in the relationship? Going through a difficult time and dealing with changes of personality are completely different. In difficult times, you both face and deal with it together, but a change in personality or character means you are on your own, unless this new personality is one you are willing to settle for lack of living your own life.

A woman needs her own life despite who or what comes and goes. When all is said and done, all you have is the Lord. I will be with you always, even unto the end. You can only be yourself, and no one can take that away from you until you allow it. You may argue and say that you are generous, but think about it: Why would you give all of you, including your mind, body, sanity, and money? What is left of you? Don't you think unless you are able to take care of yourself, there is nothing you can give to anyone. Not your kids, husband, friends, et cetera. There is one of you beautifully and wonderfully made in God's image—why not make the most of that gift? Charity begins at home, a statement we have heard all our lives. It is always easier to do wrong, but remember, someone who does not support you obviously has no love for you. We have heard it so many times: the words "I love you" taken for granted by humans. We think if it is said, there is no need for the action of proving it. You must be smart, use your head, and PAY ATTENTION! If you put the words alongside the action, there will be a clash in the meeting. The mouth will have said what you wanted to hear, blinding you from seeing the truth happening right before your eyes every day. When you have finally opened your eyes to see past the sweet smiles and small petty manipulations, wisdom will clearly reveal the drama and ridiculous nonsense you've been allowing for the sake of having someone make you feel good—when all along you had the tools within yourself to not just feel great but be great. "For my God shall supply all my needs according to his riches in glory by Christ Jesus" (Phil: 4:19).

You can accomplish anything you set your mind to if you follow through. Just a little determination goes a long way, and it is a tool to get rid of undesirable characters around you. I have always been told that when you are a certain person, you are attractive to a certain crowd. Aren't you tired of meeting inconsiderate, selfish people? Money hungry, low self-esteem, and all qualities we do not want in a husband—blame only yourself.

This is how it works: On your first date, you meet a nice man, until you see his true colours, e.g., good, his cheap. That is ok. You move on. LEARN TO MOVE ON. The next many meetings are selfish, then the next is needy, and so on. One day, you look back and wonder how you came to meet so many fools. You must look at it as lessons learnt. This is the reason! If you were paying attention from day one, you would notice that as you met each one unwanted quality, you would have been aware earlier and you have learnt the signs and will save yourself from future repeats of old mistakes.

As you go on with life and grow with knowledge, you will be customizing the list of "I DON'T WANT." Later when you have met Mr. Right and not Mr. Right now, the supposing love, and understanding and not forgetting financially, you will know and recognize it because you been PAYING ATTENTION.

Life is all about lessons to be learnt. The trouble is so many of us are just going through the motions. Another mistake we make as women is we go looking for a husband. Looking for one of those is like going looking for the flu. You will not know the strain till it is too late. One searches for a house or a car—not a husband. While you are searching for a husband, you are neglecting your goals, looks, state of mind, and spirituality. You are a university dropout or unemployed.

You have not been to the gym in months, you have lost your individualism, you have no faith, you are overly sensitive, and you have a false sense of security—better known as arrogance. Tell me what good husband will want you now? It is a good husband you are looking for, right? Have you found him yet?

Get back to the reality of being yourself that God has created you to be. Be productive, ambitious, and beautiful you, asking God to provide the husband and future he sees fit for you. Our God promised to supply all our needs according to his riches in glory.

Rescue mode

Too many times, we fall and want someone to pick us up. Others need picking up too. If everyone is in rescue mode, who does the rescuing? We know what it is to have and to have lost, but the real loss is learning nothing from those experiences. It seems we must end up flat on our faces before we are able to see. We have too much pride. Pride comes before a fall. We should learn to be rid of pride and to replace it with dignity and respect. We need to learn to embrace each error as lessons learnt so that we can make room to learn new ones. We often wonder how we got here to realize life has been taken for granted. Too often, we feel like we have it all figured out and it's all safe. We forget that constant maintenance is required for a productive life. We must learn to play continuous attention. Knowledge is power. Though it comes from reading, that is just one way. Life is the best teacher.

The Bible is a book based on life—stories told of the lives lived, the errors made, the lessons learnt, the ultimate sacrifice ever made, the highest price paid, how it all began, why it was done, and for whom it was done. "For God so loved the word that he gave his only begotten son that whosoever believeth on him should not perish but have everlasting life" (John 3:16). It is the greatest story ever told. There is nothing happening to us now in our lives that is not in the Bible. Everything that happens—good or bad—serves a purpose, so keep paying attention as it is a joyful memory, an opportunity to be patient, or a lesson to learn. The power of that information is profound. No one can make you see that until you allow yourself to acknowledge it. Someone has said to me in the past, "I can't watch when you feel sorry for yourself because it's not you." We must learn to accept weak moments (it's human nature) but learn not to allow it to ruin the day. Too often, we allow ourselves bad days. Why? All we have is today, and tomorrow belongs to no one. We need to realize that the decisions made today will affect tomorrow. Why not start now? We can do more in one month that we have done in the last year. So many of us want to discover joy and contentment, not realizing it is not out there—we must discover it within. Let us teach by the examples of our lives and for us who are learning to support and continuously fight to excel as we pull each other up. Not knowing who you are is the worst fog of life to be in.

Teach them so they can teach theirs

Why do parents feel the need to control their adult children? At some point, we all must be capable of demonstrating and proving the ideals, discipline, and values instilled into us as children. But how are we to show what we have learned if there is never allowed a time for the practical based on the theory? Parents often feel it is necessary not to let go because they do not trust that they have taught their children the responsibility to self. How is one to meet a husband or wife in life if parents insist everyone is wrong? Weren't they wrong for someone once until they learned to make better decisions? Have they forgotten what it is like to be wrong and can learn through experiences, wisdom, guidance, and pain? When you search your heart and history as a parent, can you honestly say, "I did my very best, and I have given my children the tools for a well-adjusted life without parental supervision or my own paranoia"? Have you prayed with and for them and showed them a spiritual example that they may have a clear understanding of a spiritual life and walk with God?

There is a need for confidence in being the best parent you can be. You cannot give more than you got. Teaching from a heart of love is one of the fundamentals of parenting. Our experiences are filled with lessons, and so we focus on the gift of knowledge so that we can teach them to be better than we were. We cannot pass judgement on the past experiences and fore parents because we never knew how we were going to handle what our ancestors faced, and we had no idea that with all the given circumstances, we could have done better.

We learned so that we can teach the next generation. There will be greater healing going forward, as there needs to be improvements and the breaking of old traditions that cripple us without losing the grasp of our cultures. This is how we can break some of those generational curses. Some of the ways we were disciplined with rods of correction have left many of us scarred, and we now have a generation to raise who we realized cannot be disciplined in the same methods.

We have realized that unless we unlearn the old way of thinking and relearn a better way of communicating with our children, we will be creating roadblocks instead of healthy relationships with them. We also need to guide them to ways of making wiser choices for themselves instead of manipulating their decisions. We often forget what it's like to be a child, and we can sometimes inflict our adult point of view, not realizing we are being misunderstood, not because they don't care but because they aren't us.

We are here to guide and equip our children as much as possible with life skills to be prepared for their own adventure and discovery. We cannot predetermine their lives, but we sure can create a supportive environment so they have re-enforcement for the tough part of the journey that is life.

Judgement

It is amazing how often we are so close to family, and yet we are the greatest danger to them simply because we are too busy being so perfectly godly that we fall short of realizing how judgemental we are. We focus on the good others should have done and ignore the amends that we should have made to ourselves. We see the imperfections and magnify them only to reject our own cries from within. God's call on us is not for us to magnify others' faults. However, it is a call to magnify him, deny ourselves and praise him, and to empty ourselves to him, so that he may fill us with his will for his peace.

Let us stop and surrender who we are. Let us decrease our focus on self and increase our focus on him. Only then will his grace be sufficient for us, and he will fight the hindrances in our lives for us as his plan for us happens. We can then be examples so that others can see as we bear witness of him. God will be glorified in all we do.

We will never be perfect, but completely surrendering to God continuously gives him the freedom to use us for greatness and reduces the enemies' influences in our lives.

Christ tells us that our righteousnesses are as filthy rags before Him (Isaiah 64:6). So who are we to ever look to another to think we are better?

"Man looks on the outward appearance, but God looks on the heart" (1 Samuel 16:7).

He also says in his word that he looked to find one who was worthy and there was not one.

We all are imperfect. Why do we as humans feel it is necessary to categorise sin and make it seem like some are ok and others are not? No one sin is worse than the other. Wrong is wrong—no grey areas. Never in God's word are we told that stealing a penny is ok but stealing a car is bad. If we are so good, why must we go to God every day to confess our sins and ask for forgiveness? We know not what tomorrow holds because we are only guaranteed today. How do we know the decisions made today will positively impact the plans predestined for us? We can sometimes be so lazy and indecisive that the plans for us are full of blessings and favor, but because of procrastination and disobedience, we cause another life (including ours) to fail, falter, or even be lost and not even realize it. Yet we are the one quick to judge. "Oh, I wouldn't do that if I were her. Whatever was he thinking?" we say. During numerous instances, God has looked at our lives and most definitely could have said, "You shame me" or "I expected better of you," but in all his infinite mercy, he forgave us.

The old saying "People who live in glass houses shouldn't throw stones" is not thought about enough. How about we put our stones down and look at ourselves in the mirror and not see others through our windows? Then there can be self-improvement and less of a need to throw stones. We want to do too much, say too much, and cause too much pain and conflict. Now guess what is said after all the headache? "Sorry!" Really? It is that simple, huh?

Let us try to have pounds of prevention with the almighty God as our guide. Let us worry less for a cure. It is better to work on the individual self, allowing the positive to manifest in us, and then there will be more lives blessed by example of the light shining through us from within. His light penetrates every darkness.

Too easy

Giving yourself over to the cute guy will not seal your fate with him. If he already has the bonus, why put in for a soon-to-end relationship? How many times have you seen it happen to others? What makes you so special that a guy would look and say, "Oh, she is easy—let us take her home to mama"? Why would you want to give that sacred part of you to a stranger? It's about time we realize that every time you meet someone, and it doesn't work out, it's your number increasing. Imagine if you will, three years later, and you have finally met the one you were meant to be with. Exactly how many were before? Think now. If you control yourself and refrain till you know just what you need, you will realize that there is so much to learn about character building without—you know—sex.

Why do we insist on giving up our innermost parts just because of feelings of inadequacy? What does it benefit, simply to give into a moment of bliss, without considering the implications of tomorrow? Each one of us has had an impulsive moment, but how many does a person need to realize that it is not just the moments but a pattern of behaviour? It all starts within. Everything we need to survive is already within us. It is discovered by situations, experiences, and all through life. The key is to pay attention. Some people learn early, others learn later on in life, and there are the odd few who never seem to get it. Take a moment to think of the most difficult situations you have ever faced. If you were to face that situation again, what would you do differently?

How much of your response came from hurt or anger or plain cruelty just to feel an instant sense of satisfaction? Think further on how much time you wasted on what should have been a much shorter process. Would it not have been great for you to have paid attention a lot earlier in life? We can never be spared from all heartache and pain, but we can know that the future will be brighter because God has given us the free will in our lives. Why not use the best source available to us? As we grow older, we learn to pay attention as there are always lessons to be learnt and memories to cherish. We cannot go without heartbreak, but we can become stronger and smarter simply by paying attention to everything around us. I once heard someone say that you do not have to experience the lessons—some are learnt by watching those around you. We must take advantage of those too; think of the pain you save yourself or someone else.

Busy being busy

How much free time do you have? Do you find yourself unable to add anything new to your schedule but you want to have someone to share your life with? What are you busy doing? Yet you complain that you are single and lonely, and there is no one available. How can you see who is available when you are so occupied being unavailable? You have not realized the void you are trying to fill is still empty? When you are alone at night and the day is done, did the business work? Or does the business keep you distracted from the fact that you are busy existing and not living?

When life is passing you by every second, have you ever stopped to catch your breath?

We tend to tell ourselves that we are happy being single because we have no time for someone else in our schedule. Yet at midnight, the truth reveals itself in the moment that you realize there is no one to sit down next to you and watch television or even to massage your feet. Someone to have a two-way conversation with and not a bark or purr in response. Yes, it is great having pets, but since when did animals replace human companionship?

Will that puppy, or kitten, pour you a glass of wine, have a bath with you, or massage your temples after a long day? We see the strong, driven women during the day and out in the evenings. Where is she when the drapes are drawn and reality hits? Where is she when the loneliness is evident and the truth that she conceals is hidden behind the power suit and the busy schedule?

Have you ever considered being honest with yourself instead of trying to avoid the emptiness inside that keeps eating away at you?

It takes a strength to admit to yourself that you prefer to have companionship. Embrace your true self and search to see what it is about you that dreads the thought of trying to allow another person into your personal space and into your heart. So, we have all been hurt before, but allowing that person's or persons' behaviour to prevent you from exploring the possibilities of having a full and joyous life is giving them too much power over your life. When you really give it some thought, do you want to have a has-been to be the hindrance to great possibilities? Life is not perfect, but it sure is better having the adventure in joy and sorrow with someone by your side who appreciates you. It's your life, so let the adventure begin.

Divided

Have you ever wondered why we are different people in one person? You are one personality at work because you need to prove you are not a pushover, and you're a pushover at home because you don't want to hurt anyone's feelings. Finally, when you are out socially, you are a complete flake. You are unable to have a conversation, you drink too much, and then come Monday morning, you're hoping that no one finds out.

Monday morning: You wake up and get dressed in your business face and outfit. You are aware of yourself, driven, intelligent, and accomplished. When the workday is done, you (a woman of dignity and perseverance) pay attention and are willing to share knowledge. These are some good ingredients to a successful life. None of us has all the answers, but we are blessed with trusting God and having faith. He guides us along, giving us clues throughout our lives. Too many times, we fall and want someone to pick us up. Others need a hand to get up too. If everyone is in rescue mode, who does the rescuing? We know what it is to have and to have lost, but the real loss is not learning anything from those experiences. We must end up flat on our faces before we are able to see. We have too much pride. We need to embrace each error as lessons to learn from and realize that even as we grow and improve ourselves, we will keep making more errors. Be sure to learn from each one so you won't have to have repetitive lessons.

It is the greatest story ever told: the ultimate sacrifice made on a cross by our Lord. There is nothing happening to us now in our lives that is not in the Bible. Everything that happens—good orbad—serves a purpose, so keep paying attention as it is a joyful memory, an opportunity to be patient, or a lesson to learn. The power of that information is profound. No one can make you see the lessons until you allow yourself to acknowledge it.

Someone has said to me in the past, "I can't watch when you feel sorry for yourself because it's not you."

We must learn to accept weak moments (it's human nature) but learn not to allow it to ruin the day. Too often, we allow ourselves bad days. Why? All we have is today, and tomorrow belongs to no one. We need to realize that the decisions made today will affect tomorrow. Why not start now? We can do more in one month than we have done in the last year. So many of us want to discover joy and contentment, not realizing it is not out there—we must discover it within. Let us teach by the examples of our lives and for us who are learning to support and continuously fight to excel as we pull each other up. Not knowing who you are in the fog of life is the worst place to be.

May you have come to realize that the greatest joy is to be at peace within yourself, and you are then clear to make your own decisions, which leads towards self-contentment.

You are never alone

We should give support to people so we can teach and learn even through our weaknesses. Jesus Christ uses us in every situation to teach and learn from each other. Believing you are stronger than others emotionally does not mean you cannot lean on them. It is not all about you. Where you are strongest, you get to be the support for those who are weak and vice versa. We cannot all be weak at the same time in the same areas—it would cause an onset of chaos. What good would that do?

When we have each other to lean on in moments of weakness, it strengthens us. When others see us in situations requiring help, we can work together to pull ourselves up a lot quicker than a singular effort. A strong woman carries everything, but a woman of strength handles what comes her way because she is not alone. Christ tells us, "I will not leave you, never forsake you." He is our rock and our shield.

She takes every encouragement that comes so when life brings the challenge, she is strong enough to keep moving forward. Embrace challenges because character is built in overcoming and therefore creating a resilient system. She is filled with grace, beauty, and contentment and is respected, dignified, and blessed.

Her husband is honored to call her his own and companion for life. No other woman is comparable to her in his eyes. Her children are blessed to have such guidance and teaching. Her friends are just as supportive and blessed as she is but each in their own uniqueness because God blesses us with people who will lift us up. Strangers will marvel at her glow of peace. A goal always begins with a want or wish, but not all follow through. There is nothing wrong with wanting it all in life. Just know it does not come without the grace of God and having him first in your life, and even then, he gives what is best for you with the desires of your heart. Many people want for themselves what they see in others. What is it, you ask? Joy! A glow, was it? I wonder. Find out and ask, "What?" "Why?" and "How can I?" A person with a good heart filled with joy will not keep it to themselves. She is happy to share and help others feel that way too. Jesus is the Way, the Truth, and the Life (John 14:6). He also came that we might have life and have it more abundantly (John 10:10).

There is no joy, peace, or strength of our own. The God of glory and might is the only source of limitless love, joy, peace, and contentment. In him, a heart that is hurting finds comfort. A life of sadness will be made full of joy. Women are taught to do everything with our hearts and mind. Our passion and drive are what keeps us going, but we are powered by the strength God gives. When life gets tough, we sometimes get carried away by emotions and forget who we are. We appear to be superwomen, and some of us act that way too, but we must also allow ourselves to be human. We need to remember that sometimes we will fall, and that's ok, yet the secret to success is not in the fall but how quickly we pick ourselves up.

We did not ask to be put on a pedestal nor to be seen above others. That only creates more pressure because a pedestal is perceived as perfection, so mistakes and moments of weakness seem unforgivable. No one can be harder on a woman of strength than herself. When others expect the best of you, you want to only give your best. We must recognize the humanity in ourselves and accept our faults and failures. But make no mistake about it.

We make mistakes—we are not a mistake.

Temper! Temper!

Why can't we keep our tempers in check? So, you and your husband have a disagreement—that is normal. But why do you have to put the man out of his home? Women, we often think we have the upper hand when our spouses make a silly move. If you do not want to sleep next to him after, there is nothing wrong with that. The guest room or the couch can be made available, but you cannot put the man out of his home. It is his home too. No matter the challenges being faced, throwing someone out of their home is childish. Let us suppose you decide that putting him out is the right thing to do, and unknowingly, Sally down the road has had an eye on him. He takes off only to conveniently bump into her. She is obviously sad for him and sympathetic. She offers him an innocent cup of coffee or a glass of wine, and in his vulnerable moment, he goes for it. You get up the next morning only to find him coming out of her house. You then are upset with Sally because you cannot believe she is such a home-wrecker.

If you had kept your business indoors and dealt with it in a better manner, Sally would be unaware of your marital challenges. Now on top of the disagreement, you must prevent a scandal or rumours about your marriage. We must look in the mirror sometimes to realize that as women, we do and say too much too quickly in the heat of the moment. We often need more time-outs than kids. It is easier to prevent problems than to try to fix them. Imagine that a scandal or rumours are like a bag of feathers released from the top of a building, and you're asked to get them all back into the bag. Good luck. Not a fun way to learn lessons.

Too many things can go wrong before we realize that we can be our own worst enemy. If only we could take a minute to be quiet and listen or even walk away and calm down, we could have been a lot farther in some aspect of our lives.

Sometimes when a spouse finally decides to walk away from a marriage, the reason to do so did not happen overnight. We let things fester and eventually grow into giants, and then we wonder where this comes from. There are always signs of trouble. If we look to where we have been and what we have learnt, we will realize there were signs, but we were too busy or blind to see the sign. Some women see the signs; however, they are too inexperienced to understand what it meant or only plain stubborn to their instincts and decided it was ok to ignore it this once. God has given women the gift of inner strength and compassion, and when that strength is lost, it is because we forget our source, and in that moment of weakness, we try to do everything ourselves. But without God, nothing is possible. He is our strength when we are weak, our shield in times of storms, our go-to anytime, anywhere with anything Saviour.

Say something!

Too often, we watch some women get head over heels in relationships. He has his own home and lives alone. You have your own too, but out of convenience, you spend more time at his place than your own. One day a few years later you on, you are entering your home, and it is a mess from neglect, but his is spic and span because of your hard work cleaning it. You are suddenly empty on the inside at your place, but you keep trying to convince yourself that you are happy at his home. He seems comfortable with the convenience that you've created, and you notice he's made no offer or advancement on the status of the relationship.

It is called denial. You have been settling for what he offers because you really do not think you can do better or have not realized you really do deserve better treatment than this. Unless you know your self-worth, you will always be accepting of less for yourself. This is another reason why we can do nothing on our own, for God has given us the authority with him, telling us that we can do all things through him who strengthens us (Phil. 4:13).

Men think differently than we do. If you go with the flow, then you are indirectly saying to him, "I'm ok with things the way they are." Your actions depict what others read of you. They will only know what you show. Allowing yourself to keep how you truly feel about anything will only be addressed if you communicate the truth, whether it be by verbal communication or by your action—then, you can take action based on response or the lack thereof.

I am so sorry you wanted things to turn out differently when you did not speak your mind, allowing your voice to be heard. You were, in turn, creating a bad situation for yourself, resenting him. He may not be naturally controlling, but you gave him control unintentionally. Then you want to grumble or say to your friends that he does not even know that you exist.

You said nothing—then guess what? Someone will take the reins of your life and make it theirs; you have a responsibility to yourself and to maximize the fruits and gifts God has blessed you with. Talk to yourself, pick yourself up, dust yourself off, and make your voice be heard because God sure did not make us with breath in our bodies to be idle.

Be that strong woman of virtue the Lord calls us to be and take your place in life so you won't be left behind. Let our heavenly father be our guide, surrendering ALL to him. And do we mean *all* ? Learn to surrender everything because we have a bad habit of going to God and taking all our needs and troubles to him, but just before we walk away, we turn back as if to say, "Well, I'll take just those to worry about because it needs to be done by Tuesday."

We should learn to surrender ourselves to Jesus, let his plan manifest within us, and then will we be given a spirit of boldness to be better women and a voice alongside our husbands. Even with our relationships, we must maintain our individualism and not lose ourselves in everything else. The burden for the woman is always seen as heavier to bear because we keep it all inside, not allowing the husbands to know, and then when all fails, we want to blame everyone else but ourselves. How are we to know what the outcome is? We tend to be judge, jury, and executioner in our lives.

"Well," we say, "he is so busy working, so I do not want to bother him" or "Oh, he needs his rest, so I do not want to make him stressed." We were not taught that saying nothing creates a much greater problem that often results in divorce and hate because we never gave others a chance to make their own decisions and be supportive. If, when you ask, he fails to help, then you handle it accordingly, but do not be the defender of the husband and then be the woman who is the bearer of all things who will turn into a bitter and miserable person.

This may seem like an attack, but, my lady, it is. Satan is on the attack. When anything goes wrong, it's time to be awake in the moment so we can realize and learn the lesson. God allows some things to happen in our lives to help build us up for his honor and glory, but in all aspects of life, we must never forget there is always a spiritual battle being fought. The fires and darkness of this world are continuous, and marriages failing are the enemy's plan.

Put your action into what you know you deserve. Women who allow themselves to be treated poorly are a result of low self-esteem, not knowing better, or a false sense of security. If we learn from our mistakes and pull ourselves up to represent self-respecting, emotionally and financially independent, self-maintained women, we will have more males stepping up to much higher standards of men—men with decorum, etiquette, respect, and love. (P.S. The roles can be reversed too.)

We allow too many poor behaviours in the name of love, but love is patient and kind.

Stop fighting the destiny God has called you to live. If we are going to represent him, let us do it in every aspect of our lives. We must let go of all that has passed and release ourselves of all God has already forgiven us for and move for.

We have all messed up. We want this peaceful and joyful life, but we are afraid to have it, yet Christ died for us. None of us is without fault. "For all have sinned and fall short of the glory of God" (Romans 3:23).

That is why we remember John 3:16: "For God so loved the world that he gave his only son, that whosoever believeth in him shall not perish but have everlasting life."

Do not give up who you are as it is all you have. No matter how much you try to deny it, you will only self-destruct. No matter what the day brings, God is bigger than it all. Isn't there a voice within you crying to be heard? It is saying, "I want to be me." It's all about letting Christ restore you so there can be a positive to all you do that is great. Then your life will be nourished no matter what challenges arise, and even in your moments of weakness, you will know and depend on the hope of our Lord Jesus Christ. He always comes through. "I will lift mine eyes unto the hills from whence comes my help. My help comes from the Lord which made heaven and earth. He will not suffer thy foot to be moved, he that keepeth thee will not slumber" (Psalm 121).

Beside him or over him

We are always quick to tell him when and how to be. It must be the motherly instinct. In fact, did you know that before you came along, he was managing quite fine? He is doing great—sure, because of you in his life—but I am sure that the basics were all easily done without your step-by-step instructions. Why do you insist on telling him how he should speak to people? If he has always been outspoken but polite, then leave him alone.

We forget that there is a difference between personality and mannerism; first up, your personality is who you really are: thoughts, experience, and attitude. Mannerism is how you handle situations: with rudeness or respect. For example, a situation arises where he would usually speak out, but with your suggestion in mind, he decides not to say a word. You, his lady, feel disrespected and he feels like a fool now. Sometimes we need to learn to be quiet. Often, we feel that voicing our opinion is the best, but many times, we are wrong.

He knows how to turn down the AC in the car and does not need you to give step-by-step instructions on how to do it. Who was doing his laundry before you took over, insisting he should not touch his own clothes or they will be ruined? I am sure you loved the way he dressed when you first met him. How did that finely dressed man suddenly need for you to pick out what he should or should not wear? It is one thing to suggest an idea; it is another to let him know in no uncertain terms that he is incapable of dressing himself. You are simply and quickly emasculating him. Such behaviour on your part as a woman makes your husband look like a fool.

There is nothing wrong with him letting his lady make decisions, but there is something wrong when knowledge of your husband being continuously treated as weak is shown to others. Nice being old school and with a touch of the modern. You should trust that he is capable of being a household leader, and you should try to let him. When you are blessed with a good husband, you should believe that he is a great choice, and do not doubt yourself. In every relationship, one must be able to maintain a sense of individualism and bring into that relation an air of clarity—not perfection, but a sense of knowing that each person is capable of being true to whom they are. With God at the head of it all, there will be peace and joy with you two that you are not so busy irritating each other. Then the outside chaos that you two should be facing together now won't seem so overly strenuous that the relationship becomes pointless. There is no true happiness there. How would you feel if someone spoke using the same disrespect that you do? It would make you furious. Well, what you do not realize is that you are paving the way for others to treat him. If a woman shows respect to herself and her husband always, it gives no one the authority to do otherwise. How you live your life and portray it tells others how to treat you.

Do it for yourself

What do you mean by, "I don't know how to cook"? It is said that society has led us to believe that dinner should be on the table by five. How can a woman who wants children, a home, and a husband not know how to cook? Have you heard the phrase the way to a man's heart is through his stomach? Too many women think that being knowledgeable of our restaurant menus is a great thing. When you meet your intended husband or even are just dating or courting, don't you think it is impractical to purchase every meal? Don't you think that when times or budget is tight, you will want a much more affordable method of nutrifying yourselves? Or will you simply downgrade to the fast-food menu? It's the twentieth century and yes, we are independent, yes, we know how to provide for ourselves and don't need someone to do everything financially for us, but how for and how ridiculous is it when you really think of the future with the way you think now?

Cooking, cleaning, decorating, and grocery shopping are simple fundamentals for life. You don't need a man or husband to be able to be domesticated or say, for example, you believe you should be able to afford domesticated chores to be done. Don't you think you may get tired of someone waiting on you for some of the basic things that actually give you joy to do in your own home. You especially receive gratitude from your husband and children when they see the example or self-involvement in a home. Nothing wrong with having help because boy, do we ever need an extra two or six hands in the home. But do you want the example of cleanliness and home involvement to be learned from a stranger? It also gives a sense of contentment to give small gifts such as a cake from scratch for holiday seasons or a romantic dinner or breakfast. So, you don't like scrubbing bathrooms or vacuuming, and you decided to get a professional in weekly to alleviate the pressure of

too much to do. That is different than thinking you can only eat out or
have everything done for you because you can afford to.

Do not plan problems

How many children do you want? Does he know that you are trying to get pregnant? Or is he aware that you have made the decision not to have children, but you have him believing you are trying to?

Tell me something. Will it be worth the end results when the truth comes out? Remember that everything in the dark must come to light.

Let us play the "if" game—you feel it's time to have a baby and he is not ready. No matter how many times you try to talk to him into it or to stimulate his interest, you hit a brick wall of resistance in him. What on earth would give you the idea that after getting pregnant without his knowledge, he will have to accept the fact that it has already happened and it will be ok? So you proceed with your sneaky plan. You one day announce that you are so shocked to find out that you are pregnant. He is not pleased but is calm, and you think you have won. You are so happy and are looking forward to the baby being born. He will not touch you during your pregnancy, and you do not realize he does not trust you anymore. There is continuous friction, and you get upset that when the baby is born, he is not instantly overjoyed by the birth. You cannot understand why he cannot enjoy and embrace this miracle. Within him, a raging storm of questions whirl, wondering what else you are capable of beyond this betrayal of trust. He sees you differently. Nothing wrong goes unpunished.

You cannot seem to agree anymore. You need the father for the child and the support, but all you have is a heap of responsibilities and loneliness.

Now think back—didn't he already have a family? And you figured with what you saw that it was best not to do things the right and old-fashioned way and simply manipulate lives to get what you thought would be the ideal husband. Getting pregnant was the last desperate attempt. Your body alone could not hold him, as men eventually those who grow up see past a lovely body and require more. Your constant request to have a life or give you a commitment was never responded to with the answers you wanted to hear, and so getting pregnant was the final desperate attempt to get what you thought should be yours. He had never given you the indication that he wanted a life with you, and so my question is how did you turn it to convince yourself that you should restructure his future? Manipulations never have good results. Now you have his child, and you are not having the time of your life like you planned.

Now don't get it wrong—he has his share of blame and responsibilities, but this here is about we women looking ourselves and raising our standards and expectations so those around us may follow our lead and then—and only then—by God's guidance and grace will we have more and more real men, not little boys in grown bodies, stepping up their standards. What is the point, you ask? If all standards are higher and you do not want to be lonely, then their standards and expectations of themselves will rise. But if we accept any and everything, then why would anyone want to do the work or even make the effort to earn better? Are we little girls in grown women's bodies', or are we applying every lesson learnt to each next step we take? Not one of us is free of wrongdoing. Who are we to judge, but also who are we not to pull up our fellow sisters to say, "I understand what it is to be a woman, and I will help you up in your weakness as I've been there"? And though our errors are different, the lessons in life remain the same. Let him who is without sin cast the first stone.

Some of us fail to pay attention because we are so busy keeping up appearances only to impress everyone, but eventually, the veil falls, and the truth is revealed to a desperate cry for help. We make people believe that our lives are great. Status is created, but it is all a figment of our imagination when all along, people are laughing. Do not give others such power over you. The world is filled with people to wait to see other veils fall or weaknesses revealed, and they bask in the sight of your hurt or time of trouble. It is a cold, cruel world, but God is our refuge and strength, a very present help in our times of trouble. Little girls pretend life, but real women live their lives.

Did you also think that because he strayed, that made him completely available to you? You never did. Why would you settle for a man who keeps you a secret and not choose to have someone pursue you to intrigue your interest? If you are the mistress, chances are, the future is not looking bright. There are two types of men: good ones who make mistakes and get themselves back in gear (they tend to be dependable and sought after), and then there are those, either married or single, who will repeatedly make the same mistake because it's all about their selfish desires.

We talk too much . . . too much

We women need to learn to be quiet sometimes and pay more attention to the inward woman than the external. It is difficult enough being a woman, so the last thing we need is for a moment of weakness or frustration to have whoever was within earshot to go running off your mouth. How did you feel when you incidentally had a day of stress and out comes your business with a voice of grief and exhaustion? Was it a good feeling after you had your business all over the place? Why is it that we gossip, or as we put it, "just had to share some information." We as women, and I do mean women, not little girls in grown bodies, need to sometimes keep our thoughts to ourselves. It's time we empathize in knowing how it truly feels to go through a tough time, a moment of extreme frustration, and it is a real shame that so few women are willing to admit their frustration or difficult times. To go on pretending that life is great is not good, either.

There is a difference between being secretive and simply keeping private. Secrecy is when you do not allow admittance to yourself that you have hurt or pain because you need to keep up an appearance of perfection. Privacy is cautiously selecting who you allow to share your hurt and pain because some people will rejoice to know you are hurting. They will get excited to see and know that there is turmoil in your life instead of seeing the strength God gave you to go through it and survive. They will magnify your pain just to make themselves feel better. You have to always be aware that the enemy will forever try every way to put hindrances and negativity in and around you. That is why we go to the throne instead of going to human sources. Others will see our pain and turmoil, but as we trust God to take us through the storms of our lives in our darkest and weakest moments, it is not about us, and he uses our storms to let his glory shine through us so that he may be praised. That is why we can always sing to God for the great things he has done.

When we look at the times we trusted God in our storms and allowed his will, no matter what people say, we know within our hearts that it is well. When we know or happen to hear of another's grief, how about a whispered prayer for strength in their time of need or distress? Our heavenly father will then bless us and others through us, and then his will and his kingdom will be glorified. We can celebrate triumph in the life of another woman repeatedly. Think of the greatness that could be when we allow the grace and power of God into our lives. He has made us with an unspeakable strength wrapped in gentleness.

Beauty in others

Must every compliment come our way? What is wrong with saying to someone something pleasant and respectful just to make their day? It is not all about us. We could simply say, "You look beautiful" or "That's a great outfit." It reflects in our relationships as well. You should be the one he dotes on, or your response is negative if you happen to not like the compliment because you would have worded it differently. Have you realized that everyone's mind works in its own way and process? In the relationship, when did you last give a compliment to your spouse, boyfriend, or fiancé to reflect your unselfish intentions?

A compliment should say that it is not about me, for without me, you are still capable of being an awesome person. We give the perception that we are so desperately needed in the relationship that our husbands or significant others could not tie their shoelaces without us. We give the impression that if they were to live without us that they would surely die. The world would come to an end if we were not in it.

Let us check ourselves here and list the qualities and accomplishments that were a part of him before you met. What was it that attracted you in the first place? Were you the one who instilled discipline and strived to see that he was a great person? So, what has suddenly made you believe that you are the only reason for his being?

You need to remember to compliment him but not boost his ego to the extreme but let him know that you, the chosen woman in his life, sees him for who he is. He needs to know that you are aware of him and of how appreciative you are of his contributions in helping make a life with you and your family or whatever your dynamics are. It is not suddenly all about him now, but it goes both ways, so when you feel the urge, it helps to let him know he is not alone on the journey. God is the head of it all, but human relationships were designed to be healthy, and it helps to have appreciation from both sides. It is a necessity.

You need to be aware that when he sees, feels, and knows that you have his back no matter what life brings, it will motivate him to work even harder to not fail you. It also allows you the freedom to see the true potential of your journey together, giving you the confidence to be even better at your part of the contribution in the relationship. There are some fundamental details in creating healthy communication . . . appreciation for him and from him.

Sometimes, we talk continuously to each other with nothing of value being communicated, and it can be vacant cycles of dull verbalizing. Within the relationship, each person has opportunities to display strength. It's all teamwork, as no one is always the leader. "The man is the head of the house" is a spiritual guideline and foundation creating an atmosphere of stability that leaves no doubt as to the status of the home, but in each isolated struggle and life situation, there is a revelation of strength in each person, thus giving turns to be the lead to not have every stress on one person. Years later, the strength as the couple builds into a great marriage not a perfect one. You must know the difference.

There is no such thing as a perfect anything when it comes to human nature. I often recall a poem that was as follows:

Good, better, best Never lets us rest

Until our good is better

And our better becomes our best. (by St. Jerome)

No matter how we have given our best, we could still improve to be better than what we thought was our best.

Allowing honesty but considerate self-expression creates an atmosphere of freedom to focus on the continuous uprising issues in life. There is no worse strain on a relationship than miscommunication within the couple, plus the outside issues of regular life—it is an unbearable battle. It should be the couple teamed up with God as the head of them so the battle is not in the home. The boundaries of the adversary are clear because of the lack of confusion in their lives.

Faith: Tried and true

Why do we have so much drive and motivation in the beginning of our careers? The ideas are all flowing, the dedication for longevity is expressed, and work is the priority.

The employer is thinking, *Wow, why haven't we had this type of dedication before?* This is what makes clients happy; it makes a vast difference in the growth of the business as a well-oiled machine. Everyone is on the same page so that even when there are disruptions, the responses are amiability and understanding. When the hours are long, you have volunteers because everyone is on par for the goal of the company/ business growth. The better the business, the greater the outcome and compensation for the employees.

But why do we have a time frame as to how long things should take to fall into place? We agreed in the start to be there no matter what prevails but do not have the stamina to hold on till it succeeds. We seem to be this way in certain areas of our lives. We create time frames for a perfect marriage, the perfect child, and the perfect self. I never knew there was a designated time frame for success or a scheduled time to have life fall into where we are planning to be.

If we live by faith and hope, there are times in so many situations of our lives where we need to be still and know that God is working it out. We work hard and do our best, but we can sometimes do no more in some situations and must patiently wait as the rest is out of our hands. In the same way, there are times he guides us, so we learn through the process into his plans for us.

Sometimes I find it difficult to comprehend how lacking we are in faith, but with that same doubtful spirit, we constantly say that God has a plan. It is not that we are completely doubtful—it is that we are impatient. It's our lack of complete trust and hope that we want the answer when we decide, and oftentimes, we don't realize it, but we are saying, "God, what is taking you so long?"

He knows the plans he has for our lives and still what we want, where we want it, and control of how we want. We love to tell him how to bless us and even when to do it. When it does not fall in place as we hoped, we say, "God I don't know why you don't take this away from me," not realizing he is making beauty of our ashes because we are continuous works in progress, so he is never done working on us.

I envision faith as being on the top of the highest cliff and God is my safety net if I fall. What is better than the God of all gods handling it all because we are trusting enough to release it all to him? Imagine the results. It will not be easy, but what good thing comes easy? Jesus said in his word in Matthew 17:20, "If you have faith as a grain of mustard seed, you will say to this mountain be moved and it will be moved, and nothing will be impossible for you." I often think we are afraid to prove God's true because the possibilities are endless.

If we believe and can have our faith tested, what is preventing us from seeing past the tough situations and keep pressing forward to keep discovering what is in store for us? There has been deliverance and healing in past situations, so why can't we then believe a little more? We can smile through our pain, knowing from experience that our faith worketh patience, as it is written in God's word in James 1:2–4.

Do not dwell on the problem—let's find a solution

We hear repetition of what, when, and how things go wrong. We get reminded of who is at fault, why they should be punished, and how the problem will grow. We need more people who are aware of the problem but are focused and working towards solutions. It is annoying when we mess up and are not allowed the space to work on learning the lesson that the situation is teaching.

The naysayers are a constant nag and distraction, causing many people to get lost in the situations, and they are unable to find the lesson and survive to the point of redemption. We are so quick to find fault and remind each other of the mistakes made along with every shortcoming, maximizing our insecurities and at the same time making sure to drag someone down too. We read in God's word in Romans 3:23, "For all have sinned and come short of the glory of God."

Why are those with the most to hide the first to point out all flaws? Belittling another person especially as women we deal with the same fights in many ways. Yet when those who have judged others have their situations brought to the light, they expect mercy.

It is time we reflect on improving individualism and work on being better with each day that we are blessed as God destined us to do.

Let us have more compassion, knowing and remembering that we, too, have our own self-improvements daily. It is out of all of our imperfections and turmoil that character is built. As its problem comes to its end as nothing lasts forever and even the problems will pass, we then look back and hopefully have survived it having gained more wisdom and awareness. It will also help improve our attitude, and in many cases, we will find the situations will be handled sooner and perhaps better because the focus isn't just on what's wrong. We should instead ask, "What did I contribute to cause this?" or "What is to be learnt here and what is the solution to grow from here?"

We are connected

Are we truly lonely? Is it loneliness in our hearts or are we physically lonesome? Aren't we spending our time together? What do we really mean when we say, "I'm alone" because I am thinking, you bought gas this morning—were you alone at the gas station? We travel on the train but stick headphones on and crank up the volume.

Who served you your coffee today? Who cashed your groceries, and even when you chose self- checkout and the machine for assistance, who cleared the error? At work, who did you pass on the way in? Did you bother to say "good morning," or did you even respond to the colleague who greeted you?

You moved into a new neighborhood. How many people have you met, or are you still so stuck to your friends in the old district that you haven't even bothered to get to know your new neighborhood? Who is your neighbor? Do you know at least one, or are you going to find out who they are in case of a need or emergency? How unfair.

We are so busy being busy that we slowly confine ourselves to our own space in the middle of a crowded world and we miss it all. If we are all in this world together and are to love one another, let us think of the seclusion we create for ourselves.

We live in our minds alone and forget to pay attention to the outside world that, although it's filled with chaos and strife, it also contributes so much to our lives: a whole lot of goodness and lessons and self-improvements that we are now deprived of.

The positive is there, so let us try not to only see the negative, the chaos, and the hardship. For it is out of the chaos and hardship that comes our betterment and self-growth with self-confidence and valuable lessons. Do not be dependent on the media because it is informative with much-needed news, good and bad, but so is the National Geographic channel. Add variety to your life, know your options, and try to make choices beneficial for a blessed life. Taking it all in is not a bad thing, but you have to learn to pick the meat from the bones. It is your life, and God has given us the freedom of choices, but it is for us to choose wisely. Do not just live in your head—the variety adds to development in your life. Be physically aware and live in the moments, feeling and appreciating the goodness.

Broke, but not broken

We have at some point known what it is like to be without, whether it was no food or money, friends, or family, or even comfort in a desperate situation. It is an undesired feeling. No one chooses to be without the necessities of life, be it physical, emotional, or tangible. But if you are reading this, it means that you have been through some situations and are nodding right now. It is a gut-wrenching feeling to be in a place in your life where you feel hopeless and desolate.

To be without the earthly necessity does not mean we are without life's vital needs. How did you feel when you could not afford to buy some much-needed food or clothing? Did you fall apart because it was not available when you thought it should be supplied or provided? Did you figure a way to make do? Didn't you? You were broke, but not broken. To be broke is temporary, but to be broken is a far deeper loss and one that only God can fix. We are so fragile as humans, and he must be our shield to build our resiliency. It is a terrible feeling of shattered dreams, falling apart as you can never be put together again—it's a cry so deep that you know there's blood in your tears and no one will understand.

But as you read this today, you realized no matter how hard and impossible the situation was, you have survived it. Why can't we remember the achievement from the hard work or the victories over struggles? Our Lord Jesus promises us that he will never leave us nor forsake us. Our lives thus far have proven that he has taken us through the fire, but it has not burned us. If we can read these lines today, we are able to reflect to see that we have survived so much hurt and pain, so many difficult times, and hurtful people to be here today. It is not of our own accord, but it is because of the grace and mercy of Jesus Christ that we have made it this far to be grateful and of sound minds. Some of us take a long time to get here, but when we begin to unwittingly lean on Jesus and acknowledge that he is our rock and our everything, there is no telling where life will take us and how far God will bring us if we keep surrendering to him. Our Lord Jesus died on the cross to cleanse us of our hurt and pain and free us from all guilt and shame. I do not want that sacrifice to have been in vain. I want my peace of mind. What about you?

Don't you get tired of being tired? Tired of feeling that you need to find a way to fix your hurt. But the price has already been paid—the blood has already been shed for you to have salvation and to have abundant life. No one said it will be easy, but you can know that you will never be alone again with the unconditional love of God and peace that surpasses all understanding. I want that. I got tired of trying and failing by myself. I got tired of being tired. So, I decided to accept the offer Jesus made me. John 8:36 says, "If the Son, therefore, shall make you free, you shall be free indeed." I wanted my freedom.

Self, Mother, Wife

It is an unsaid expectation in many cultures and some families that when you get to a certain age, you need to be dating. It could be family, friends, or just your own need to do the expected thing before you hit that time line in age. When you meet him, it is followed by pressure to chase him down the aisle or make him want to take you down the aisle before he changes his mind. You need to be charismatic enough to not scare him away because it is not your idea, but in your heart, you genuinely want to make sure this is for life despite the outside pressure.

It is one thing trying to compete or measure up to the expectations of society, so imagine the pressure of those who are nearest and dearest to you. Through the pressures and coaxing, the proposal comes, "Well, don't you dare take too long to plan the wedding, or you will be asked what's taking so long."

Now the wedding day is here, and the dust settles, or so you think. Huh! Here comes the next train of push as to when are you going to have babies.

When the babies are here, you are then left alone so the pressure can be moved onto the next unsuspecting victim (the next single daughter or niece).

Then there are the cases with no expectations and no precise traditional trend to follow, so everything is at will. There is the possibility of a full career with no marriage and no children due to too many bad examples witnessed. Another possibility is pregnancies with no prospect for marriage, not because she does not want to but because she realized he has no intention of committing to having a family but is freely making mothers of his victims. These are some of the scenarios that are a reality and are the stories of some of our lives. It helps to explain why God designed sex for marriage—and for marriage to be loving, committed, and lifelong relationships between a man and a woman. He never designed it for one man to father children to various women and feel he has no responsibilities to them. Women do share the adult responsibility of motherhood but not when the man uses force, manipulations, deceit, et cetera.

We are getting older and wiser as a modern generation to see so many situations and are determined to break those generational curses and live better examples through healing for our innermost parts and wounds.

No one taught us what to be aware of while dating as there are always signs. If only we were taught to be patient enough to find out in time, we would see those indications and know to step back or move forward with those we meet. Each person met that did not work out is a lesson learned, and it's another behaviour or character to avoid, saving yourself repetitive mistakes. For example, if the date was cheap—possible signs are asking you to pay for a meal that he invited you to or asking you to split the bill after the check arrives. Avoiding the bill when it arrives so to save face he decides to cover it is another behaviour. Bad manners and arrogance displayed to the servers during your meal show he thinks he is better than others.

We need to learn to pay attention so that we are able to see the red flags of unhealthy attitudes.

During the dating stages, we need to learn money and finances. Not enough couples are taught or get to learn about sharing responsibilities while being self-sustained and continuously contributing to each other in the relationship.

My dad always taught us to know what you want from the beginning of the relationship. If you are both going to work, let it be a joint decision, so the house cleaning, cooking, and children do not seem like a burden to your spouse, who works too. I did not realize the truth of it till I learned the hard way.

Have a conversation as to how soon you both want to have children so that you are not blindsided with pregnancy when you have not had a chance to know your husband. No one can explain the difference that comes with dating and being married even though you may have been living together prior to the marriage. Couples need time—especially young couples who have not lived together. I am not saying it should not be done because there are the exceptions who know from day one just what they want and when.

That place

How do we get to that place that feels like no return? So far gone into that negative place we never planned or saw coming. You do not recognize yourself nor are you able to pull out of it. There is a sliver of hope left, but it is so faint that it is not enough to rely on yourself.

Something or everything feels wrong. Your stomach has that huge knot, giving you a nonstop feeling of hopelessness. Your choices right now are not familiar because they seem like the end to all you have earned and hoped for. You begin to dig deeper, feeling that sliver of hope is going to build into something bigger and greater again. Now comes that feeling of desperately not wanting to feel this hurt. Your self-doubt is overwhelming, but at this point, there is nowhere else to go but up because you refuse to keep feeling this sense of lacking, and failure has never been an option for you.

When you have aimed to not allow the setbacks in life to change your perception of a positive and hopeful future, it will be a bit, but you will find your way, especially when no matter how low things fall, you have the rock to lean on. The sliver of hope is your constant connection to Jesus. He is the one source of dependability, and even when we drift from him, he will see us through as he promised never to leave us nor forsake us. He said in his word that he will take us through the fire of our lives, but the fire will not burn us (Isaiah 43:2). We are testimonies to his deliverance because no matter what, we have made it this far. James 1:2–3 says, "My Brethren, count it all joy when we fall into divers temptations; knowing this, that the trying of your faith worketh patience." We have to learn to appreciate the tough times because it's through them that we are built and taught patience.

Overly independent

How often do you know that you should say no to a request, but because you are so strong and capable of handling it yourself, you say, "Yes, it's ok. I got it"?

We believe that if we do not do it ourselves, it will not be done correctly. A confident and independent woman knows that she wants a husband in her life but is also fully aware that she does not need him. Wanting him does not change who she is: It adds to her as marriage should be as designed by God. She does not need a man to stay with her for the sake of her children, and neither should she be with him for their sake. She would rather he leaves or, stranger yet, she'll be gone with her children.

She believes in teamwork, and she is willing to give 100 percent and wants him to give his 100 percent. It is not always fair in life, but she can roll with the ups and downs. She is in no matter what comes but, of course, there are boundaries. God gives us boundaries. Who are we to give unlimited access to be eventually run over and worn out?

She is human and is so aware of her own weakness that she sometimes, or even most times, is willing to take on the leading role. She needs her own independent man at her side too.

She starts by never saying "no" just so things get done or "yes" to just get some things moving. She gets busier and busier, thinking her husband will just jump in to do his part. What she does not know is that if he has not been taught or told, he could not read her mind to know what she needs him to do.

There is an expectation that develops in humans when others continuously take over to just allow them to do it all. It is what happens when you realize that you will not get him to voluntarily be a better partner and that he is limited by his selfish needs because he never learned better.

Now she is doing everything because she keeps saying, "I got it." But does she?

These are the situations one can get into when we make decisions during our stages of pain and in the process of growth and evolving. She comes to realize that in spite of the choices that she made back as the person she used to be, she cannot live this way anymore, and now she realizes she has to make decisions for the person she is becoming.

Evaluate your tears

So, you left him. My question is this: Why are you crying? Allow yourself to feel the emotions of pain and embrace the feeling of freedom. Do not feel guilty. How many times have you tried to get out of this relationship? You have been trying to leave with his permission. Which controlling spouse or boyfriend will allow you to leave? Eventually, you started realizing that it's your own permission and no other that is needed for decisions in your life so you can have a future without having the same fight over and over again.

It just happened to be the first time you've succeeded in your twenty times of trying to leave, and each try has made you stronger. Now your eyes are open, your conscience is clear, and your mind is free. Your eyes are opened to see that the person you were when you made the decision to be in this relationship has now matured and evolved into the woman you are developing into. Your goals have changed, and so has your outlook on the future. Your conscience is free because you have gone above and beyond to do your best, but it was never enough. Your honest efforts were squandered by unappreciation and neglect. But you are now starting to see it was not the other person in the relationship, but you are the one who was in the wrong place and wrong relationship. At some point, it stopped working and you decided you can fix it because you are already there and that you believe in loyalty. You never considered that it was your sign for an exit to your next stage of growth. Staying in a relationship when it is nothing but friction is a red flag saying that it's time to re- evaluate your life.

Your mind's now free. It takes a while. It depends on how long you were in that relationship and how deep you were in—you will have to allow yourself that healing process. You may be gone physically, but the emotional detachment will be all up to you and how much you chose to push forward to gain strength and resist the temptation of old habits.

You will find yourself crying, but you must keep reminding yourself that God sees every tear you cry, and he is into healing broken hearts. Admitting to God that your heart is broken helps you to embrace the healing.

Misplaced hope

We keep hoping in humans and keep being disappointed, but hope in God is peace. We need to see the proof in humans as the Bible tells us that by their fruits you will know them.

How is it that we put so much trust in the wrong places? I believe we have to create healthier boundaries in our lives. There are individuals with whom we have no right to create intimate relationships, such as business colleagues or associates. It is the reason why so many work atmospheres are toxic due to misplaced trust.

Let us explore this idea. If we decide to allow ourselves to trust a new meet with, say, 5 percent of trust at a time and if the individual does not disappoint, then we can release a bit more trust. It allows us to create the boundaries of knowing who is allowed minimum access to us, and we will with patience realize those who can be trusted in different areas of our lives. Boundaries are necessary, and not everyone should have full access to every area of our lives. It is a sensitive subject, and it will definitely guide us in seeing the difference between those we work with and live with, those we share our thoughts with, and those we only listen to.

Stepping out

I am working on continually believing in myself and following through with accomplishing what I want—not fearing what I do not want. Because my focus is to be the best me, I can be as God destined it, and that is my priority. So, I focus on a happy home with my kids. I have it. It comes with its challenges, but I will pick the normal day struggle I have over the gut-wrenching mental battles I had. That is my experience. I could not stay in a place of constant battle and wonder which way to go. I had to take the dive into the unknown with faith as my grasp. I was desperate for a change and so sick and tired of everything else not working. My life, my choice, my decision. So, I leaped. I stepped out of my comfort zone and decided to do things I have never done before and some I had not done in an awfully long time. I took a chance on me for my children and my future.

I could not expect a promise or guarantee to know what to do. All I knew is this:

This has been my anthem. When I am in doubt, I remind myself repeatedly that I am stepping out of the old mentality. I could not live like that anymore. I will take a small apartment with me trying my best and doing good all by myself than to have any other human being stress me out. I DESERVE BETTER!

I am experiencing clarity with emotional and mental freedom. I hope you allow yourself to feel the pain and go through the process—no matter how painful it is. It is better to do the mountain climb and make it to the top than to stay in the valley and live with the illusion. I want the mountaintop experience, and no matter how many valleys I go through, I refuse to lose and stay down.

Remember that every mountain had a valley, some wider and deeper than others. The higher that mountain, the deeper the valley, so start climbing because you are not alone. You must also know that not every battle is yours and that you must learn to surrender them to God so you can enjoy the peace that he gives as he handles your battles for you (Exodus 14:14).

God has promised us that all we need is faith the size of a mustard seed. It does not take much. Let us step out with that leap of faith. Any movement forward is a step in the right direction. No matter how slow, it is better than no change or no movement forward.

Boundaries

Life teaches us so many lessons, and what we take or give back reflects what we learned. The resilience we have is based on the levels of victories that we have overcome. It prepares us for the future and helps us make different choices, if not better choices. Boundaries are from some of the best lessons learned in situations and relationships. They are meant for the right place and the right time, so you are protected within reason and balance. Some boundaries are to protect you from manipulative people, and some are to prevent you from crossing between professional and personal lines. There is a difference in boundaries when crossing relationship lines into friendships.

Do you know when to create the right boundaries? You may ask, "How are we to know what the right type of boundaries is and when to apply them?"

If we look around, we will realize that there are those who make such extreme efforts to forget the past, but we need to reflect and remember lessons of the past because it reminds us of the signs and red flags. That's one of the ways to help create some of those much-needed boundaries.

What are your boundaries made of? Are your boundaries set by you, or are they determined by the strength of the opponent or situation? Are your boundaries pliable like straw, and it takes little for you to be knocked over or overwhelmed? Does it take the small, sweet manipulations to turn your head from the decisions that are best for you?

Are your boundaries like bricks or titanium, like great walls around you every day and everywhere? No one could get in or out. What are you afraid of so much that you are hard on the inside and blocked on the outside? You cannot prevent hurt or tragedy by avoiding living. How do you know you are not missing out on the best that's available for you if you run from everything, thinking you are afraid of the results? If you know nothing of what tomorrow brings, how can you not want to try to discover the possibilities?

About the Author

Julietta Raoul

Hi, I'm Julietta Raoul, and I'm from St. Lucia. I have been writing since I was a teenager as a way of clearing my mind. This book was originally thoughts of situations that I've either experienced or witnessed. It's heartbreaking to see the number of women who are silently suffering with the belief that no one else will understand situations that they are facing or the shame of things they have done.

There is also a societal pressure and traditional expectations that nullify our individualism. We are told who to be and how to be, and when it does not work out, the result is abandonment as if we did not follow a manual correctly.

I have had to learn the hard way, and that can be devastating. Finding my voice late in life did not feel like I did not get to live. As a matter of fact, I found an unexplained level of gratitude for God's grace bringing me through all I have survived. I have had to learn to love myself, embracing how uniquely we are created. We are like no other despite similarities. I have also tried to stay in the shadows because I was sure I was a misfit yet always stuck out like a sore thumb. I was afraid of how I expressed myself and was intimidated by my own thoughts. They always seemed like ideas too big for reality. I was always told as a child that I needed to be seen and not heard. I was suppressed for so long that when I got my breakthrough, it felt like a rocket bursting forward from the deep hole.

I stopped fighting my purpose and was finally free. I realized that I am not quiet or shy and that I am an artist with many talents.

Discovering my purpose has made me enjoy helping other women accept their scars and be ok to grow past them. I believe that every scar is part of our growth and makes us stronger.

If we can remind ourselves of all that God has brought us through, we will see the grace that is always there for us to lean on to persevere into the future. My dream is to add to the lives in which I come into contact.

All fear does is hinder our progress.

I believe in our growing together, even when we have our own time and pace.

Excel with me or get out of my way!

Acknowledgements

This is dedicated to my family, friends, and mentors. You know who you are.

I could not have been here without you. Thank you for your love and support. This book would not be possible if God had not blessed me with you all. I appreciate you!

Lightning Source UK Ltd.
Milton Keynes UK
UKHW011905290621
386364UK00001B/20/J

9 781649 697523